THE PORTABLE 7 HABITS™

Vision

Defining Your Destiny in Life

THE 7 HABITS
OF HIGHLY EFFECTIVE PEOPLE®

Other Portable 7 Habits Books
Choice: Choosing the Proactive Life You Want to Live
Purpose: Focusing on What Matters Most
Abundance: Fulfilling Your Potential for Success
Trust: Sharing Ideas, Insights, and Understanding
Synergy: Connecting to the Power of Cooperation
Renewal: Nourishing Body, Mind, Heart, and Soul

Other Books from Franklin Covey
The 7 Habits of Highly Effective People
The 7 Habits of Highly Effective Families
The 7 Habits of Highly Effective Teens
The 7 Habits of Highly Effective Teens Journal
Daily Reflections for Highly Effective Teens
Daily Reflections for Highly Effective People
Living the 7 Habits

Loving Reminders for Kids
Loving Reminders for Couples
Loving Reminders for Families
Loving Reminders Teen to Teen
Loving Reminders to Make Kids Laugh
Quotes and Quips

Franklin Covey
2200 West Parkway Boulevard
Salt Lake City, Utah 84119-2099

Concept: Cheryl Kerzner
Design: Jenny Peterson
Illustration: Tammy Smith
Written and compiled by Debra Harris
Contributors: John Crowley, Ann Hobson, Sunny Larson, Shelley Orgill

Manufactured in United States of America

ISBN 1-929494-10-6

CONTENTS

The best work we can all do is create the highest vision possible for our lives and be led by that vision to the greatest good.

—OPRAH WINFREY

INTRODUCTION

In order to land your dream life, you need to make a conscious effort to visualize it happening. However, keeping your eye on the prize takes practice. It's all about getting rid of misconceptions about yourself, giving up emotional baggage, and putting a new belief system into place. The premise is pretty simple. All it takes is the desire to figure out what you want and the determination to make it happen.

In *Vision: Defining Your Destiny in Life*, we've simplified the powerful principles behind *The 7 Habits of Highly Effective People* by Stephen R. Covey to help you realize your vision of the future.

There are no roadmaps to follow. No instructions. No how-tos. And no formulas for success. Instead you'll find a collection of contemporary quotes, provocative messages, and practical wisdom in an easy-to-read format.

As you turn these pages, take the words of advice to heart, mind, and soul. Think about what you read. Ponder how and what it would take to live a more fulfilling life. Let the wisdom inspire you to take a chance on happiness. To dream big and to manifest your vision, inspiration, and purpose. It's just a matter of realizing your life has significance, setting your sights on what you want, and truly believing that you deserve it.

In essence, make it a habit to begin with the end in mind.

HABIT 2: BEGIN WITH THE END IN MIND®

Defining your mission and goals in life.

VISION

To begin with the end in mind means to start with a clear understanding of your destination. It means to know where you're going so that you better understand where you are now and so that the steps you take are always in the right direction.

—STEPHEN R. COVEY, *The 7 Habits of Highly Effective People*

If you can
SEE IT
you can
HAVE IT.

What resonates in your soul?

Imagining what you want
as if it already exists
opens the door to letting it happen.

—SHAKTI GAWAIN

Start each day by seeing it the way you would want it to be. See yourself handling every responsibility peacefully and effectively. Trust that even when the results you desire do not show up immediately, they will eventually show up. See yourself moving through the day with a smile on your face and joy in your heart.

—IYANLA VANZANT

START WHERE YOU ARE

visualize it   **make a map**

write it down

plan it out

clear out the baggage

look for meaning

walk the talk

act "as if"

focus on it

pay attention

create it

affirm it

see it happen

believe and you'll achieve

Life is a mystery to be explored, not a problem to be solved.

—ANONYMOUS

You do not need to know how you're actually going to achieve a goal when you set it. Just repeatedly visualize the desired results, and

the "how" will open up to you.

—VINCE PFAFF

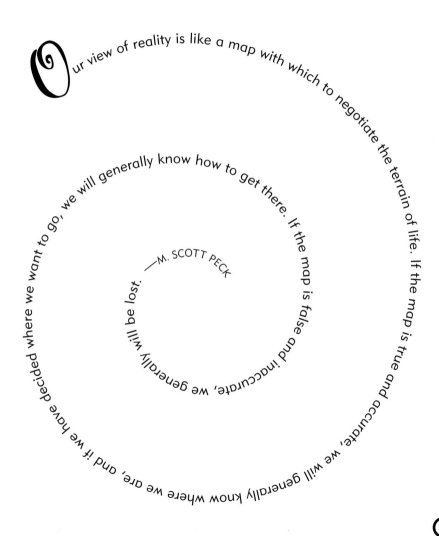

Our view of reality is like a map with which to negotiate the terrain of life. If the map is true and accurate, we will generally know where we are, and if we have decided where we want to go, we will generally know how to get there. If the map is false and inaccurate, we generally will be lost.

—M. SCOTT PECK

You can't just dream about success.

You have to

wake up

and do something
about it.

1

When you begin, don't second guess yourself.

2

When you plunge, do it wholeheartedly.

3

Ask yourself, "When is the right time to do this?"

4

Make the plunge without a safety net
other than trusting your ability.

5

Remind yourself that without taking the plunge,
your life will stay the same.

—HAROLD R. MCALINDON

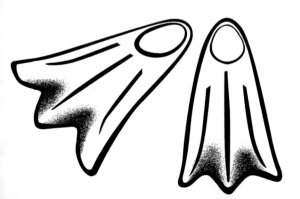

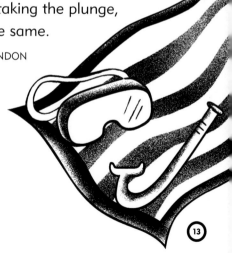

What is now proven was once only imagined.

UNDERSTANDING

When people seriously undertake to identify what really matters most to them in their lives, what they really want to be and to do, they become very reverent. They start to think in larger terms than today and tomorrow.

——STEPHEN R. COVEY, *The 7 Habits of Highly Effective People*

But now all I need in order to have a future,

is to **design a future I can manage to get inside of.**

—FRANCINE JULIA CLARK

Learn

from others' mistakes because
you will not live long enough
to make them all yourself.

—ANONYMOUS

Life is for most of us a continuous process of getting used to things we hadn't expected.

—MARTHA LUPTON

You can't understand others until you understand yourself.

*T*onight, when you lay your head on your pillow, forget how far you still have to go. Look instead at how far you've already come.

—BOB MOAWAD

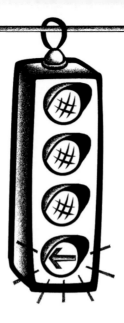

Hey, happiness is not settling for less, but just not

being miserable with what is. I have always lived

by the creed, "It's not the approval or accolades

or possessions that make you smile, but simply

making the left turn even though you were the

third car in the intersection."

—DENNIS MILLER

I read and walked for miles at night along the beach, writing bad blank verse and searching endlessly for someone wonderful who would step out of the darkness and change my life. It never crossed my mind that that person could be me.

—ANNA QUINDLEN

I will tell you that there have been

no failures in my life. I don't want

to sound like some metaphysical queen,

but there have been no failures.

There have been some

TREMENDOUS LESSONS.

—OPRAH WINFREY

You learn something new every day. Actually you learn something old every day. Just because you just learned it, doesn't mean it's new. Other people already knew it. Columbus is a good example of this.

—GEORGE CARLIN

INSTINCT

We are more in need of a vision or destination and a compass (a set of principles or directions) and less in need of a road map. We often don't know what the terrain ahead will be like or what we will need to go through it; much will depend on our judgment at the time. But an inner compass will always give us direction.

—STEPHEN R. COVEY, *The 7 Habits of Highly Effective People*

What have people been telling you all your life?

Don't bother being
NICE.

Being popular and well-liked is not in your best interest. Let me be

more clear; if you behave in a manner most pleasing to most, then

you are probably doing something wrong. The masses have never

been arbiters of the sublime, and they often fail to recognize the

truly great individual.

—JANEANE GAROFALO

A highly evolved use of intuition is being able to find meaning in symbols and synchronicities. The more we focus on finding meaning for ourselves in "chance occurrence," the more we increase our intuitive powers. Deepening our connection to our current surroundings increases our ability to follow the guidance of our inner purpose. **ALL THINGS ARE CONNECTED.**

—CAROL ADRIENNE

Listen to your
INNER VOICE.

It is the only one that matters.

Contrary to the rationalists hooey that

dreams aren't real (you're just dreaming),

dreams are very real.

They convey real information, real impact,

and real emotions, and they have real

consequences if ignored.

—GREGG LEVOY

Learning to trust our intuition

is an art form, and like all

other art forms, it takes

practice to perfect.

—SHAKTI GAWAIN

31

Everything you perceive—

everything **you sense**, or **remember**,

or **feel**, or **dream**, or **intuit**, in short, everything you

notice—**has meaning.** Everything.

—LAURA DAY

The quieter you become,

the more you can hear your ideas connect.

Often intuition will direct you. If it feels right, it's probably right.

—OPRAH WINFREY

FOCUS

As we go deeply within ourselves, as we understand and realign our basic paradigms to bring them in harmony with correct principles, we create both an effective, empowering center and a clear lens through which we can see the world. We can then focus that lens on how we, as unique individuals, relate to that world.

——STEPHEN R. COVEY, *The 7 Habits of Highly Effective People*

The
world
doesn't
come
to the
clever
folks,
it comes
to the
stubborn,
obstinate,
one-idea-at-a-time
people.

—MARY ROBERTS RINEHART

Think about something that you want but you believe is impossible to attain. Challenge your negative thinking for the next 30 days by acting as if you've already attained it.

Prepare to be amazed.

It is only by following your deepest instinct that you can lead a rich life, and if you let your fear of consequence prevent you from following your deepest instinct then your life will be safe, expedient, and thin.

—KATHERINE BUTLER HATHAWAY

The world asks

that we focus less on how we can coerce something to

make it conform to our designs and focus more on how

we can engage with one another, how we can enter into

the experience and then notice what comes forth. It asks

that we participate more than plan.

—WHEATLEY AND KELLNER ROGERS

What would make you

deliriously
happy?

When we have lost ourselves, no amount of externals will help. Spouses, friends, work—none can supply what is missing when we are cut off from our "internal power source." We are missing, and the only way to remedy this problem is to find ourselves again. Finding ourselves takes time. It is hard work and it is worth doing.

—ANNE WILSON SCHAEF

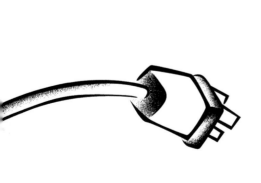

Get Focused

1. Give up the woulda-shoulda-coulda routine.

2. Forget the past. It won't matter next week.

3. Stop being crazy busy. It's an energy drain.

4. Take time for yourself. You deserve it.

5. Assume there's a reason for what's going on.

6. Eliminate unneeded distractions.

7. Forget about what other people think.

8. Quit beating yourself up over small things.

9. Forget the no-margin-for-error mindset.

10. Breathe.

When you decide to explore what would make you feel happy, fulfilled, secure, joyful, and confidently challenged, try to focus on the feeling that you ultimately want to experience...

Keep it simple.

How do you want to feel? Keep your focus on being led to the perfect opportunities that allow you to be happy, to be of service in attunement with your abilities and desires, and to be well rewarded.

—CAROL ADRIENNE

KEEP A JOURNAL

of your hopes, dreams, goals, and accomplishments. If your life is worth living, it's worth writing down.

*L*iving well is an art which can be developed. Of course, you will need the basic talent to build upon: they are a love of life and ability to take great pleasure from small offerings, an assurance that the world owes you nothing and that every gift is exactly that, a gift.

——MAYA ANGELOU

CREATION

Through imagination, we can visualize the uncreated worlds of potential that lie within us.

——STEPHEN R. COVEY, *The 7 Habits of Highly Effective People*

Creators start at the end.

First they have an idea of what they want to create. Sometimes this idea is general, and sometimes it is specific. Before you can create what you want to create, you must know what you are after, what you want to bring into being.

—ROBERT FRITZ

When in doubt,

make a fool of yourself.

There is a microscopically thin line

between being brilliantly creative

and acting like the most gigantic

idiot on earth. So...leap!

—CYNTHIA HEIMEL

49

The ultimate creative act is to express what is most authentic and individual about you.

—EILEEN M. CLEGG

The Creative Thinker's
SWEET SIXTEEN

1. Choose to live a creative life.
2. Make creativity a daily habit.
3. Capture your ideas.
4. Take intelligent risks.
5. Have fun with your ideas.
6. Be yourself.
7. Act on your creative urges.
8. Keep feeding your mind.
9. Stimulate your senses.
10. Create from your passion.
11. Take a daily step toward your dream.
12. Have an idea-friendly place to create.
13. Keep creative resources nearby.
14. Have creative companions.
15. Learn from your mistakes.
16. Never give up.

—HAROLD R. MCALINDON

Never stop feeding your brain.

The first step to being creative is to get rid of your own unwritten rules.

—MARY M. BYERS

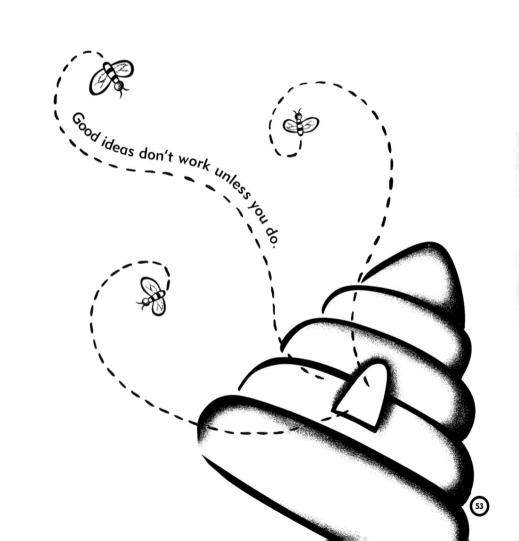

Good ideas don't work unless you do.

THINK

When was the last time you had a big idea and acted on it?

To stay ahead, you must have your next idea waiting in the wings.

—ROSABETH MOSS KANTER

55

Because of the routines we follow, we often forget that life is an ongoing adventure. We leave our homes for work, acting and even believing that we will reach our destinations with no unusual event startling us out of our set expectations…Life is pure adventure and the sooner we realize that, the quicker we will be able to treat life as art: to bring all our energies to each encounter, to remain flexible enough to notice and admit when what we expected to happen did not happen. We need to remember that we are created creative and can invent new scenarios as frequently as they are needed.

—MAYA ANGELOU

If creative thought processes are blocked,

OPEN-MIND SURGERY IS NEEDED.

MISSION

The most effective way to begin with the end in mind is to develop a personal mission statement or philosophy or creed. It focuses on what you want to be and to do and on the values and principles upon which being and doing are based.

—STEPHEN R. COVEY, *The 7 Habits of Highly Effective People*

Do you live up to your potential each day?

It is not possible to get all our definitions from outside and maintain our spiritual integrity. **We cannot look to others to tell us who we are,** give us validity, give us our meaning, and still have any idea of who we are. When we look to others for our identity, we spend most of our time and energy trying to be who they want us to be. And we are so fearful of being found out. We truly believe that it is possible to make others see what we want them to see, and we exhaust ourselves in the process.

—ANNE WILSON SCHAEF

It seems to me that we are on some mission to discover every deep-rooted reason for being unhappy. We employ sophisticated therapies to plumb the depths of our very psyches. The first thing it seems people have difficulty grasping is the simple premise that life often just is not fun. Okay, I suppose the pursuit of happiness seems ofttimes almost as tragic and futile a gesture as the loading of the ice-making machine onto the Titanic.

—DENNIS MILLER

A personal mission isn't **AVAILABLE AT A STORE NEAR YOU.**

LIFE'S DEFINING MOMENTS

1. FIND YOUR PASSION

What do you care about most? Create an overview of what drives you and what you could do without. Allow your passion to take more priority in your life.

2. FOLLOW THE BIG PICTURE OF YOUR LIFE

Don't waste time on things that aren't important or that don't become part of the big picture. Allocate your time more efficiently.

3. SPELL OUT TO YOURSELF A DREAM VERSION OF YOUR PASSION

How does it feel? What does it look like? Where would it take you?

4. GET A MOVE ON

Don't wait until a better time to move toward what you want. There is no better time. The time is now.

5. STAY OPEN TO CHANGES

Just because things aren't going exactly to plan doesn't mean they are not in alignment. Trust the process.

May the road rise up to meet you.
May the wind be at your back.
May your mission in life
feed your passion like no other.

Most people spend their lives struggling along the same old road, wondering whether they will ever reach their dreams. The lucky ones discover there's a beautiful six-lane expressway just over the hill, created just for them. It's their personal path, ready and waiting to speed them to their dreams.

—CHRIS J. WITTING JR.

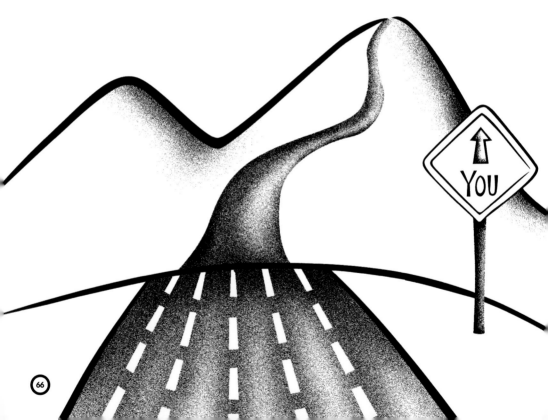

HOW TO WRITE A WORKING
MISSION STATEMENT

Write down a list of things you love to do. Make a second list of positive attributes about yourself. Start with the words "I am..." Make a third list of things that you want most in your life. Here are some additional list ideas:

What do I keep gravitating to?

What did I like to do as a child?

If I could change anything what would it be?

What interests me most right now?

What do I like most about myself?

What fills my soul?

What can I do well?

What are my most unique traits?

Compare and contrast all your answers. Combine them in ways you never considered. Somewhere in there is your true mission in life. Use these words to write a personal mission statement. If the words feel flat and unexciting, you're on the wrong track. If they overwhelm you with emotion or excitement, you're on to something!

There's always a way to find the time, and if the mission is right, the money will be there. The issue is to

have the heart
and the courage to move ahead,

to have the courage to take one step forward and know that will open up doors to new levels of well-being.

—GREG ANDERSON

If
you had to,
could you give
it all up to
realize your
mission in life

Here is the test to find whether your mission on earth is finished.

If you're alive, it isn't.

—RICHARD BACH

CENTER

By centering our lives on timeless, unchanging principles, we create a fundamental paradigm of effective living. It is the center that puts all other centers in perspective.

——STEPHEN R. COVEY, *The 7 Habits of Highly Effective People*

Center is a state of being.

You are centered when you are moving on purpose, without irritation or

frustration. You are centered when you are

open to discovery,

no matter what the circumstances, when you are

willing to learn and to change

based on what you learn.

—JUDITH S. WARNER

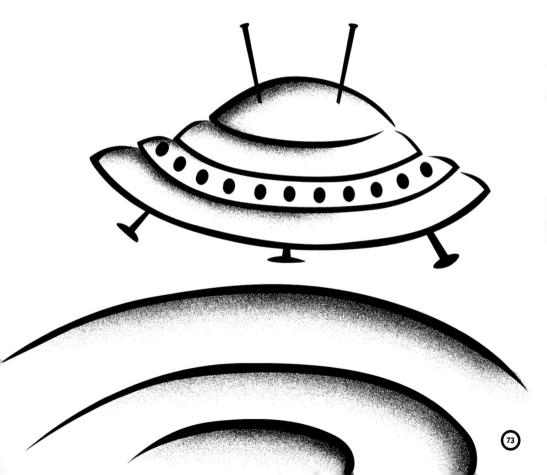

YOUR EGO HAS LANDED.

How Centered Are You?

1. **When you hear the word "center" you think of:**
   (a) The tallest basketball player on the team.
   (b) The last word in left-of- or off-. (c) It's all about being balanced.

2. **Your idea of living a balanced life is:**
   (a) Mixing Flintstone vitamins and Tums with Calcium. (b) Owning a satellite dish without any sports channels. (c) Having your cake and eating it too.

3. **When you listen to your intuition you hear:**
   (a) The chaos theory. (b) Hip hop. (c) Answers.

4. **In order to live in harmony and balance you'd need to:**
   (a) Become an airy-fairy, crystal clutching, mantra humming New Age type.
   (b) Supersize a value meal at your favorite Scottish restaurant.
   (c) Find a path that works for you and stick with it.

5. **How often do you reflect upon your vision or purpose in life?**
   (a) Never. My only vision is to see Elvis reappear at the local Piggly Wiggly.
   (b) Rarely. I have a right to be dysfunctional and nourish my inner martyr.
   (c) As often as I can. It helps me stay focused and on track.

Mostly a answers: You're just skimming the surface of life. A little more depth would do your body good. Open your mind to the possibilities. And ditch the negativity. Remember, you are what you think you are.

Mostly b answers: See mostly a answers.

Mostly c answers: You're on your way to living a balanced life. That doesn't mean you follow a strict plan without ever going with the moment, however. You're balanced enough to know it's all about learning, not about being perfect.

CENTERING IS

"the Zone"

SPOKEN OF BY GREAT ATHLETES.

It can also be a barefoot run on the grass on a summer's eve,

with the wind in your face and the senses wide open...It is like a

delicate flower growing out of solid rock. Center can be a cosmic

laugh rippling out to the ends of the universe. It can simply be

relaxing in rush-hour traffic. Center is returning home. It is

always a choice we can make.

—THOMAS CRUM

Each day I examine myself on three counts: whether or not I am **loyal** to those in whose behalf I act; whether or not I am **trustworthy** in my dealings with friends; whether or not I **practice** what is imparted.

—TSENG TZU

I Know I Am Centered When...

I am balanced and stable.

I am breathing deeply from my belly.

I am relaxed, calm, and focused.

I am aware, internally and externally.

I am appreciative of myself and others.

I am feeling my emotions—and learning from them.

I am compassionate and connected to others and to my environment.

I am able to receive and give sincere acknowledgment.

I am energized by purpose.

I am bigger than my challenges.

I am unattached to the outcome of a situation.

I am having fun and laughing often.

—THOMAS CRUM

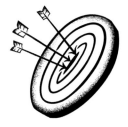

Do not be concerned about others not appreciating you.
Be concerned about your not appreciating others.

—CONFUCIUS

VISUALIZE IT

Close your eyes and breathe deeply. Reflect upon something that you're holding onto that's not working anymore. What would your life look like without it? What one small step can you take to let go of the attachment? How would it feel?

There's a bit of magic in everything, and some loss to even things out.

—LOU REED

WISDOM

Our wisdom and guidance comes from correct maps, from the way things really are, have been, and will be.

—STEPHEN R. COVEY, *The 7 Habits of Highly Effective People*

Everyone is born a genius,

but the process of living degeniuses them.

—BUCKMINSTER FULLER

When you're young, you don't know, but you don't know you don't know, so you take some chances. In your twenties and thirties you don't know, and you know you don't know, and that tends to freeze you; less risk taking. In your forties you know, but you don't know you know, you may still be a little tentative. But then, as you pass fifty, if you've been paying attention, you know, and you know you know.

Time for some fun.

—GEORGE CARLIN

WISDOM
is not a fad.

Nobody grows old merely by living a number of years. We grow old by deserting our ideals. Years may wrinkle the skin, but to give up enthusiasm wrinkles the soul.

—SAMUEL ULLMAN

We are well-advised to keep on nodding terms with the people we used to be, whether we find them attractive company or not. Otherwise they run up unannounced and surprise us, come hammering on the mind's door at 4 a.m. of a bad night and demand to know

who deserted them, who betrayed them, who is going to make amends.

—JOAN DIDION

By the time you figure it out

YOU'LL BE SO OVER IT.

A
finished
person
is a
boring
person.

—ANNA QUINDLEN

Too many wish to be happy before becoming wise.
—SUSANNE CURCHOD NECKER

CRITICISM

is just someone else's opinion.

It's possible to have too much in life. Too many clothes jade our appreciation for new ones; too much money can put us out of touch with life; too much free time can dull the edge of the soul. We need sometimes to come very near the bone so that we can **taste the marrow of life** rather than its superfluities.

—JOAN CHITTISTER

One cannot have wisdom without living life.

—DOROTHY MCCALL

DESTINY

We are responsible for our own effectiveness, for our own happiness, and ultimately, I would say, for most of our circumstances.

—STEPHEN R. COVEY, *The 7 Habits of Highly Effective People*

Destiny isn't a matter of chance. It's a matter of

CHOICE

The future is the time
when you'll wish
you'd done what
you aren't doing now.

ONE OF THE GREATEST JOYS IN LIFE

IS TO BE IN SEARCH OF ONE THING

AND TO DISCOVER ANOTHER.

—ANNE WILSON SCHAEF

When dreams die,

life is a broken-winged bird that cannot fly.

—LANGSTON HUGHES

I believe that when all the dreams are dead, you're left only with yourself. **You'd better like yourself a lot.**

—RITA MAE BROWN

KEEP the LESSON

throw away the experience.

*O*nce a king built a great highway and invited his people to see who could travel the highway best. On the first day, people who traveled the new road complained to the king that a large pile of rocks and debris had been left and the mess hindered their travel. One lone traveler, tired and dirty, handed the king a bag of gold, explaining that he had stopped to clear a pile of rocks that blocked the road and found the gold. The king gave the money to the man, saying, "You've earned this gold. He who travels the road best is he who makes the road smoother for those who will follow."

—UNKNOWN

What we seek we do not find

—that would be too trim and tidy for so reckless and opulent a thing as life. It is something else we find.

—SUSAN GLASPELL

What we most want to run from we'll end up running toward and drawing to us, the way sharks are attracted to thrashing bodies.

—GREGG LEVOY

If you're climbing

the ladder, make

sure you know

what wall it's

leaning against.

If we were supposed to be perfect, spell check wouldn't have been created.

AFFIRMATION

Through imagination, we can visualize the uncreated worlds of potential that lie within us.

—STEPHEN R. COVEY, *The 7 Habits of Highly Effective People*

Affirmations for the Soul

We said, if we're going to do a book, then let's have a mega best-seller. Your mind works based on programming, and so what we said is that we'd program each of our minds independently. As we went to sleep, we'd say "Mega best-selling title, mega best-selling title." We'd say it 400 times, because we needed a perfect title for the book...we'd give ourselves a thought command saying, "It's going to come to one of us at 4 o'clock." Jack was the blessed one, he woke up, got goosebumps and said, "Chicken Soup for the Soul!" He called me in the middle of the night and we had the title...We went to New York to sell it, and 32 publishers said, "That ain't gonna make it, that's too nicey-nice. Sixty million books later, I think it might make it."

—MARK VICTOR HANSEN AND JACK CANFIELD

The **most important words** we'll ever utter are those words we say to ourselves, about ourselves, when we're by ourselves.

—AL WALKER

DIRECTIONS: One affirmation in mirror each morning. Repeat affirmation as necessary. Use daily for best results to relieve symptoms of negativity and doubt.

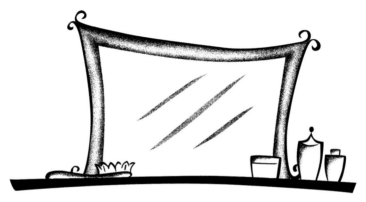

I will meet someone new today.	I can do this.
My world is full of new experiences.	I am lovable.
I am strong and healthy.	I am a success.
I will not be stressed today.	I can achieve my goals.
Whatever happens, I can deal with it.	I am happy and free.
I will help others today.	I am loved.

I will overcome this. It's just an obstacle in my path.

Daily affirmations are an important way to
pick yourself up.

We all have our bad days and you can't always count on other people to make things better. For instance, you might say to someone, "I'm a bad person," expecting them to say in return, "Oh, no, you're not, you're one of the kindest, most thoughtful people I know." But nine times out of ten, they'll say instead, "Really. H'mmm. Hey could you pass the Chee-tos?" And sometimes you're not even eating Chee-tos, you're eating barbecue potato chips or some weird flavored popcorn.

—ELLEN DEGENERES

SAY GOOD-BYE
TO YOUR
INNER CRITIC.

Well, here's another clue for you all: The walrus

was an affirmation. What? What I mean is that

even the best medicine in the world won't work if you don't take it. And as a

nation, we don't like to take our medication. We are all

naughty Randall McMurphys, slipping our pills under our

tongues, thinking we are beating Nurse Ratchet. Talk about

shooting yourself in the psychological foot.

—BEN STILLER

To say something nice about themselves, this is the hardest thing in the world for people to do. They'd rather take their clothes off.

—NANCY FRIDAY

Self-respect cannot be hunted.

It cannot be purchased. It is never for sale. It cannot be fabricated

out of public relations. It comes to us when we are alone,

in quiet moments, in quiet places, when we suddenly

realize that, knowing the good, we have done it;

knowing the beautiful, we have served it;

knowing the truth, we have spoken it.

—WHITNEY GRISWOLD

Our deepest fear is not that we are inadequate. Our deepest fear is that **we are powerful beyond measure.** It is our Light, not our darkness, that most frightens us. We ask ourselves, who am I to be brilliant, gorgeous, talented, fabulous? Actually who are you not to be?

—MARIANNE WILLIAMSON

About Franklin Covey

Franklin Covey is the world's leading time management and life leadership company. Based on proven principles, our services and products are used by more than 15 million people worldwide. We work with a wide variety of clients, Fortune 500 material, as well as smaller companies, communities, and organizations. You may know us from our world-renowned Franklin Planner or any of our books in the 7 Habits series. By the way, Franklin Covey books have sold over 15 million copies worldwide—over $1\frac{1}{2}$ million each year. But what you may not know about Franklin Covey is we also offer leadership training, motivational workshops, personal coaching, audiotapes and videotapes, and *PRIORITIES* magazine just to name a few.

Let Us Know What You Think

We'd love to hear your suggestions or comments about *Vision: Defining Your Destiny in Life* or any of our Portable 7 Habits books. All seven books in the series will be published in 2000.

www.franklincovey.com/portable7

The Portable 7 Habits
Franklin Covey
MS0733-CK
2200 West Parkway Boulevard
Salt Lake City, Utah 84119-2331 USA

1-800-952-6839
International (801) 229-1333 Fax (801) 229-1233

PERMISSIONS

RECOMMENDED READING

Adrienne, Carol. *The Purpose of Your Life*. Eagle Brook, 1998.

———. *The Purpose of Your Life Experiential Guide*. Eagle Brook, 1999.

Bragg, Terry. *31 Days to High Self-Esteem*. Peacemakers, 1997.

Canfield, Jack, and Mark Hansen. *Chicken Soup for the Soul* series. Health Communications.

Covey, Stephen R. *The 7 Habits of Highly Effective People*. Simon & Schuster, 1989.

———. *Living the 7 Habits*. Simon & Schuster, 1999.

Crum, Thomas. *Journey to Center*. Simon & Schuster, 1997.

Day, Laura. *Practical Intuition*. Broadway Books, 1996.

Fritz, Robert. *The Path of Least Resistance*. Fawcett Columbine, 1984.

Gawain, Shakti. *The Path of Transformation*. Nataraj, 1993.

Kabat-Zinn, Jon. *Wherever You Go, There You Are: Mindfulness in Everyday Life*. Hyperion, 1994.

Levey, Joel, and Michelle Levey. *Living in Balance*. Conari Press, 1998.

Levoy, Gregg. *Callings: Finding and Following an Authentic Life*. Harmony Books, 1997.
McAlindon, Harold R. *The Little Book of Big Ideas*. Cumberland House, 1999.

Nhat Hanh, Thich. *The Miracle of Mindfulness*. Beacon Press, 1987.

Patterson, Ella. *1001 Reasons to Think Positive*. Simon & Schuster, 1997.

Peck, M. Scott. *The Road Less Traveled*. Simon & Schuster, 1978.

Redfield, James. *The Celestine Prophecy*. TimeWarner, 1993.

Schaef, Anne Wilson. *Meditations for Women Who Do Too Much*. HarperSanFrancisco, 1990.

VanZant, Iyanla. *One Day My Soul Just Opened Up*. Fireside, 1998.

Warner, Judith S. *From Chaos to Center*. Aiki Works, 1999.

Witting, Chris, Jr. *21 Day Countdown to Success*. Career Press, 1998.